When Time Shall Be No More:
The Ultimate Surprise

When Time Shall Be No More: The Ultimate Surprise
ISBN: Softcover 978-1-955581-15-8
Copyright © 2021 by Eli Landrum

All rights reserved. No part of this book may be reproduced or transmitted in any form or by any means, electronic or mechanical, including photocopying, recording, or by any information storage and retrieval system, without permission in writing from the publisher.

All Scripture quotations are from the CSB Study Bible (Christian Standard Bible) by Holman Bible Publishers, Nashville, Tennessee, 2017.

Parson's Porch Books is an imprint of Parson's Porch *&* Company (PP*&*C) in Cleveland, Tennessee. PP*&*C is an innovative organization which raises money by publishing books of noted authors, representing all genres. Its face and voice is **David Russell Tullock** (dtullock@parsonsporch.com).

Parson's Porch *&* Company *turns books into bread & milk* by sharing its profits with the poor.

www.parsonsporch.com

*When Time Shall Be No More:
The Ultimate Surprise*

To Barbara,

my partner-in-life for more than 55 years, whose love, support, and encouragement have meant everything to me

Contents

Introduction 11
The Setting or Context 16
Parable or Literal Depiction? 20
Final Separation 23
    Matthew 25:31-34
Jesus' Standard for Judgment 29
    Matthew 25:35-36
Addendum 51
Truths for Reflection 54
Selected Bibliography 59

"It is appointed for people to die once—and after this, judgment" (Hebrews 9:27).

"We must all appear before the judgment seat of Christ, so that each may be repaid for what he has done in the body, whether good or evil" (2 Corinthians 5:10).

Introduction

Many years have passed since the event took place, but it has remained indelibly imprinted in my memory. I have revisited it from time to time, for it gave me much-needed confidence and remains a milestone in my journey as a person and as a preacher. It also remains as one of my most stressful experiences.

I was a graduate student in seminary, and I was acting as an assistant fellow for one of my New Testament professors. His classes were so large that his fellow could not handle the load. A fellow was a graduate student who graded students' test papers and passed them on to the professor for review. Depending on a student's test scores, a fellow was liked or disliked.

The student body at the seminary could select a set number of their peers to speak in chapel during the school year. At some point in my work as an assistant fellow, several students in the class decided to campaign to have me selected for the honor, and they succeeded. I want to be clear that the reason they worked to promote my selection was not my popularity; I definitely was not popular. In addition, their reason was not my skill as a preacher, for none of them had ever heard me preach. At that point, I supply-preached occasionally, but I was by no means polished. Their reason for their campaign had to do with revenge, plain and simple. The leading perpetrators wanted to see me sweat under the stress of preaching to an audience made up of seminary professors and aspiring theologians, some of whom were already pastors of churches.

The instigators succeeded beyond their wildest dreams. From the moment I learned I had been "elected" until I finished preaching the sermon I had labored over for weeks, I dealt with unrelenting pressure. I do not remember how I settled on the sermon's Scripture text, but I do remember firming up an outline as I sat in a worship service in my church. That I did so in that setting indicates how thoroughly the looming ordeal consumed my thoughts. As my pastor preached, my mind was occupied with my all-too-swiftly approaching day of reckoning. In the ensuing days, I researched, wrote, and polished.

Finally, the time to deliver arrived, and it might as well have been an execution date. I trudged to the administration building and met the Old Testament professor in charge of chapel that year. Together, we walked my "last mile" to the chapel. What followed would have been humorous had I not been more nervous than I had ever been. The professor and I met the professor presiding over chapel that day—the New Testament professor for whom I was grading papers. I probably groaned inwardly. How much more stressful could this experience become? Then the two professors began to discuss who would introduce me. It was almost as if they were about to play "rock, scissors, or paper," with the loser having to introduce me. Finally, the Old Testament professor won, so my professor did the introduction. I don't remember a word he said. I was totally concentrating on what I was about to say.

I delivered my sermon without collapsing and with no major flubs. If what my college speech professor once told us was true, my nervousness had issued in a passable performance. He told us that if we were nervous as we began to speak, we would do well because that indicated the adrenalin was flowing, which would help us. (Throughout my many attempts to preach, I held on to his statement, even though I have never been sure whether it was based on scientific fact or was his invention.) After the chapel service, a number of the people in attendance came by and shook my hand, some offering compliments. I was simply relieved to be rid of the pressure I had been under for too long. I was grateful to have survived without embarrassing myself. I went to my dorm room, changed into work clothes, and went to my part-time work, celebrating not having fallen on my face.

Sometime later, during a Sunday School class session in my church, affirmation came like "a bolt from the blue." Several members were seminary students. During our discussion of the lesson, the conversation somehow turned to seminary chapel messages. A fellow graduate student who, unlike me, attended chapel regularly, remarked that the two best sermons he had heard were delivered by another graduate student—and by me! I was absolutely stunned because I had heard the other man's sermon and did not remotely consider myself to be in his league. My fellow student's words gave me much-needed confidence in myself, which to that point I had a difficult time generating.

As I look back, I cannot resurrect how the sermon idea came to me. My best guess is that one of my professors had covered the Scripture passage in a graduate seminar on the Gospel of Matthew and had impressed on me the words' enduring importance and seriousness. In any event, I chose Matthew 25:31-46. This passage is one of several depictions of final judgment Jesus gave in the Gospel of Matthew.

In 13:24-30,36-43, Jesus gave what has been called the parable of the wheat and the weeds. To stress the truth that ultimate judgment is God's prerogative and will eventually occur, Jesus told the story of a man who sowed good seed in his field. During the night, an enemy came and sowed seeds of weeds in the field. When the landowner's servants discovered what had happened, they reported their find to him and asked whether they should pull the weeds. The landowner directed his servants to wait until the harvest to separate the wheat from the weeds. In explaining the parable to His disciples, Jesus said that at history's culmination, "the Son of Man will send out his angels, and they will gather from his kingdom all who cause sin and those guilty of lawlessness. They will throw them into the blazing furnace where there will be weeping and gnashing of teeth. Then the righteous will shine like the sun in their Father's kingdom" (Matthew 13:41-43).

In Matthew 13:47-50, Jesus presented another parable on the subject of final judgment. In what has been called the parable of the net, Jesus compared judgment with a large net that was cast into the sea and gathered various kinds of fish. When the net was dragged to shore, the fishermen separated the good fish from the worthless ones. Jesus said that at history's culmination, angels will separate righteous people from evil ones.

The evil ones will be cast into hell—"the blazing furnace" (13:50).

In Matthew 25:31-46, the basis of judgment is surprising and shocking, for it is not at all what Jesus' hearers expected—and it is not what we might expect. Perhaps Jesus' surprisingly simple yet firm, unequivocal words may be at least part of the reason the passage is so seldom visited and taken to heart. In the years following my preaching ordeal, I have delivered the sermon in a number of churches, but I have seldom heard or read other messages using that text. That is not to say that other preachers have not treated it, but my guess is that the passage rarely is explored. More treatment, I think, has been given to Paul's emphasis that "we will all stand before the judgment seat of God (or Christ)" (Romans 14:10) and what has been called "the great white throne judgment" in Revelation 20:11-12. I believe that in considering the subject of judgment, we need to begin with the words of Jesus.

The Setting or Context

In Matthew 21:23—23:39, Jesus was in the Jerusalem temple. The religious leaders challenged His authority to teach there, and Jesus not only skillfully countered their question but also told several parables that warned against the terrible consequences of rejecting God's revelation in Him. Some Pharisees and Sadducees, two prominent sects within Judaism, asked Him loaded questions—questions designed to trip Him up and discredit Him in the people's eyes. Jesus' responses, however, made the leaders look bad. The Pharisees tried to salvage some credibility by asking Jesus which of the Ten Commandments He considered to be the greatest. He correctly answered by quoting Deuteronomy 6:5, substituting the word "mind" for "strength": "Love the Lord your God with all your heart, with all your soul, and with all your mind" (Matthew 22:37). Then Jesus said a second Commandment was coupled with the first: "Love your neighbor as yourself" (Leviticus 19:18; Mathew 22:39). By the term "neighbor," Jesus meant all the people we encounter in life's daily give-and-take.

Abruptly, Jesus asked a question of his own. What did the religious leaders think about the Messiah they expected? Whose son would He be? They responded that He would be David's son. Jesus then quoted Psalm 110:1, in which David wrote that God addressed David's Lord (the Messiah). Thus, the Messiah was not David's son but His Lord. Jesus' response put a permanent end to further questions.

After a lengthy denunciation of the Scribes' and Pharisees' hypocrisy in Matthew 23, Jesus lamented over His people's refusal to accept God's self-revelation in Him (and by inference, God's offer of redemption by grace). They stubbornly refused Jesus' loving overtures and faced disaster.

As Jesus and His disciples were leaving the temple, the disciples directed His attention to buildings in the temple complex (Matthew 24:1). To curry favor with the Jews, in about 20 B. C. Herod the Great, the Roman ruler of the area that included the promised land, began a lavish enhancement of the Jerusalem temple. The main edifice was completed about two years later. The additional buildings and large courts were completed in A. D. 64. Thus, construction was in progress when Jesus and His disciples were exiting the temple complex. Jesus' response to the disciples' evident awe the buildings generated was to predict the temple's destruction, which sadly occurred in A. D. 70.

Jesus and His disciples ascended the Mount of Olives, where Jesus sat down—a teacher's normal posture (Matthew 24:3). The disciples asked Him three questions: When would the temple be destroyed? What would be the sign of His return? What would be the sign of history's culmination? In the disciples' minds, the destruction of the temple would mean the end of everything. In an extensive section 24:4—25:30, Jesus dealt with the disciples' questions. He first warned against the coming of false messiahs and then gave indications of the beginning of the end—signs that have marked all periods of history (24:4-8). He seemed to stress constant readiness in every age. In 24:9-14,

Jesus predicted that His followers would be persecuted, and some professed believers would turn away and turn against one another. False prophets would arise, and the love of some professed followers would cool. Believers who persevered would be saved, and the gospel would be proclaimed to the whole world. Then the end would come.

In 24:15-28, Jesus seemed to deal with two events: the destruction of Jerusalem and His return. He stressed that the city's destruction would not be the end; much lay beyond that event. Again, His followers were not to be deceived by false messiahs. His second coming would be as sudden as lightning streaking across the sky.

Jesus said His return would be cataclysmic; His coming would be majestic and would demonstrate His power as Deity. At that time, all His followers would be gathered (Matthew 24:29-31). Using the image of a fig tree's sprouting leaves, Jesus warned the disciples to be alert to indications of the destruction of Jerusalem and the temple, which occurred in A. D. 70 (24:32-35). In 24:36-44, Jesus emphasized that only God knows the time of Jesus' return. That return will be sudden and unexpected and will involve the separation of faithful and unfaithful people. The disciples (and all believers) were to live in constant readiness.

Using the image of a servant's being given the responsibility of overseeing his master's household, Jesus emphasized the imperative that His followers were to render consistently faithful service during the time before His return, when He would be physically absent. When He suddenly and unexpectedly returned, wicked, abusive, and self-indulgent servants would face punishment (24:45-51).

With the parable of the ten virgins awaiting the bridegroom's walk to the wedding banquet (25:1-13), Jesus emphasized the necessity of preparation and readiness as His followers awaited His return. They were to remain alert. The parable of the talents (25:14-30) stressed that while believers awaited Jesus' return, they were to invest themselves in His service; they were to risk themselves—the currency of their lives—in an effort to gain a return for Him: people who would place faith in Him. Suddenly and almost abruptly, Jesus focused on a chilling facet of His return: final judgment. He will return in majesty and splendor as the divine Redeemer and King (25:31). He proceeded to give a surprising, shocking basis on which people will be judged.

Parable or Literal Depiction?

Interpreters have suggested several approaches to Jesus' words in Matthew 25:31-46. Some view it as a parable, pointing to "the use of a simile in v. 32 ('as a shepherd separates') and a metaphor in v. 33 ('the sheep and goats')."[1] In this view, the passage would be Jesus' fifth and culminating parable, following the preceding four parables. A second approach is that the passage is a literal depiction of final judgment, pointing out that from verse 34, Jesus' words seem to give a literal description.[2] A third view is that the passage "is haggadah (illustrative stories and poetry similar to those in the Jewish Babylonian Talmud) as much as parable."[3] Frank Stagg wrote that verses 31-46 emphasize the world's fate. He stated that the section beginning at 24:1 "includes the parable of the sheep and the goats, but it is more than a parable. In its wholeness it is a prophetic picture of the final judgment awaiting all people. Emphasis falls upon the standard or principle of judgment, which is one's true relationship to Christ as reflected in his ministry to the

---

[1] Craig L. Blomberg, "Matthew" in *The New American Commentary*, vol. 22, p. 375.

[2] Blomberg, p. 375.

[3] *Holman Illustrated Bible Dictionary*, p. 1556; George A. Buttrick, "The Gospel According to St. Matthew" in *The Interpreter's Bible*, vol. 7, p. 562.

least of his people, especially in their situations of need." [4]

Worth noting is that whether Jesus' words were intended to be literal or a parable, the chilling truth is clear. As the writer of Hebrews stated, "It is appointed for people to die once—and after this, judgment" (Hebrews 9:27). Jesus' parables presented spiritual truths in story form, using people and elements drawn from everyday life. They were infinitely more than entertaining stories; each one called for decision, as though Jesus asked: "What do you think, and what will you do with this truth?" Thus, whether verses 31-46 are literal or a challenging story, the truth is clear and stark, and we must take it seriously.

I confess that Matthew 25:31-46 is one of a number of passages I could wish were not in the New Testament because they make me extremely uncomfortable. A second is Matthew 7:21-23, in which Jesus declared: "Not everyone who says to me, 'Lord, Lord,' will enter the kingdom of heaven, but only the one who does the will of my Father in heaven. On that day many will say to me, 'Lord, Lord, didn't we prophesy in your name, drive out demons in your name, and do many other miracles in your name?' Then I will announce to them, 'I never knew you. Depart from me, you lawbreakers!'

I believe the law He had in mind was the Commandment to love neighbor as self, which issues in positive action on their behalf. Standing before Him,

---

[4] Frank Stagg, "Matthew" in *The Broadman Bible Commentary*, vol. 8, p. 226.

I cannot present the many sermons I have preached, the countless Sunday School lessons I have taught and written, and the Bible-based books I have written. The crucial factor will be whether I implemented God's will, a crucial part of which is caring ministry to people in need.

Final Separation
Matthew 25:31-34

The New Testament repeatedly affirms that Jesus will return and that His return will mark the end of human history. In Matthew 25:31, Jesus stated that "the Son of Man" will come again. Throughout His public ministry, He consistently referred to Himself as the Son of Man, a carefully chosen term that served a crucial purpose. Until the final stage of His ministry, He avoided the title "Messiah." The Jews predominantly expected a military-type Messiah in David's mold who would drive out the hated Romans and restore the nation to power and prominence. Some looked for a priestly Messiah, but most expected a conquering Deliverer. In order to avoid the unwanted baggage the term Messiah carried; Jesus chose the phrase Son of Man as a self-designation. The phrase emphasized His Deity and His humanity. In His earthly ministry, instead of being a conquering hero, He took on the role of the Suffering Servant who would give His life to provide redemption. (See Isaiah 52:13—53:12.)

Jesus said He will come "in his glory." The word glory may include splendor, but I think much more is involved. His Deity will be unmistakable, as will His character as redemptive. He will be accompanied by "all the angels." Angels are a created order of spiritual beings. The word angel means "messenger." Angels are God's servants who do His bidding. As a created order, their number is set; it does not increase. As much as we would like to think otherwise, infants and young children—and even some adults—who die do not become angels. I am convinced Christians enter God's immediate presence and experience His eternal care but do not enter the set angelic order. God's servant-messengers will accompany Jesus when He returns, much as a king's retinue.[5]

Jesus' declaration that at His return He will "sit on his glorious throne" is a strong assertion of His sovereignty and majesty. He died the death of a criminal or an insurrectionist; at His return He will be Ruler with absolute authority. During His earthly life, He was the Redeemer who did not come to judge people but to save those who placed faith in Him. In John 3:17-19, Jesus said: "God did not send his Son into the world to condemn the world, but to save the world through him. Anyone who believes in him is not condemned, but anyone who does not believe in him is already condemned, because he has not believed in the name of the one and only Son of God. This is the judgment: The light has come into the world, and people loved darkness rather than the light because their deeds were evil." In John 12:46-48, Jesus said: "I have come as light into the world, so that everyone who believes in me would not remain in darkness. If anyone hears my words and doesn't keep them, I do not judge him; for I did not come to judge the world but to save the world. The one who rejects me and doesn't receive my sayings has this as his judge: The word I have spoken will judge him on the last day." At His return, Jesus will act as supreme Judge. Whether or

---

[5] John A. Broadus, "Matthew" in *An American Commentary on the New Testament*, vol, 1, p. 508.

not He will sit on a literal throne, His Deity in terms of authority, royalty, and redemptive character will be evident.

When Jesus returns, "all the nations will be gathered before him" (Jesus, verse 32). That is, all people will come into His presence. The word nations has drawn varying interpretations: (1) One view is that the term designates Gentiles. In truth, the Greek word was used to refer to non-Jews. This approach insists that what is in view is Gentiles' being judged for their treatment of Jews. (2) A second valid meaning of the term is people in general. This interpretation suggests that all people will be judged by the standard Jesus went on to clearly present.[6] (3) A third approach is that Jesus had pagans in mind: people who had never heard the gospel.[7] This view implies that these people will be saved by their works. I am convinced the second view is the correct one: All people will stand before Christ to be judged by their treatment of other people, especially people in need. Each individual will be so judged.

Jesus used a familiar scene from everyday life in Palestine. At the end of each day, shepherds would gather their flocks and separate their sheep from their goats. They could do this easily and quickly, for the sheep were white and the goats generally were black. Jesus decidedly did not indicate any shade of discrimination in the figure He used. At a point in my

---

[6] Marvin R. Vincent, *Word Studies in the New Testament*, vol. 1, p. 135.

[7] Fred D. Howard, "Matthew (Part 2)" in *Bible Bok Study Commentary, July, August, September 1988*, p. 87.

tenure as an editor of adult Bible study materials, a lesson explored Matthew 25:31-46, and one of our writers mentioned the animals' coloring. An African American who used our materials wrote a critical letter in which he protested that labelling the goats black in color offended him; to do so was racist. I wrote him and assured him that the writer stated a matter of fact to describe the scene and had no intention of expressing prejudice. In fact, "goats were highly prized in Semitic lands, and a man's wealth was reckoned by the number of goats in his flocks. There was no prejudice against them."[8] Thus, as a shepherd separated his flock, so Jesus will separate people into two categories.

Jesus said that at His return He would place the sheep on His right and the goats on His left (verse 33). According to Craig L. Blomberg, " 'his right [hand]...' refers to a place of honor; the 'left' hand to a place of disgrace."[9] The phrase "on his right" literally is "from his right" and gives the picture of a row that extends outward.[10] The same, of course, will be true for the goats, who will fan out to the left.

The sheep symbolized the redeemed, "perhaps because of their helplessness and absolute dependence on the shepherd."[11] The suggestion that Jesus chose sheep to

---

[8] Malcolm O. Tolbert, *God News from Matthew: A Layman's Commentary on the Gospel of Matthew*, vol. 2, p. 213.

[9] Blomberg, p. 376.

[10] Vincent, p. 135.

[11] Tolbert, p. 213.

represent His genuine followers because the sheep's wool made them more valuable than goats seems less likely to me. During His ministry, Jesus referred to Himself as the good Shepherd and to His genuine followers as His sheep. In John 10:11, He said: "I am the good shepherd. The good shepherd lays down his life for the sheep." He repeated His role as the good Shepherd and added: "I know my own, and my own know me" (10:14). He stated that He had additional sheep to bring into His fold, indicating Gentiles who would respond positively to the gospel. The good Shepherd who gave His life for all people will come as Judge to separate all people who have lived.

In Matthew 25:34, Jesus switched from the title "Son of Man" (verse 31) to the title "King" to indicate His sovereign authority to judge. As absolute Ruler, He has absolute authority.

Fred D. Howard pointed out that "this judgment will not be to determine who are saved and who are lost. One's eternal destiny is determined during his lifetime....Rather, the judgment described here will be for final assessment of eternal rewards and punishments."[12]

To the sheep (the saved) Jesus will say: "Come, you who are blessed by my Father, inherit the kingdom prepared for you from the foundation of the world" (verse 34). Jesus' summons demands close examination. The word "blessed' translates a Greek

---

[12] Fred D. Howard, "The Gospel of Matthew: A Study Manual" in *Shield Bible Study Series*, p. 85.

term that means "to be well spoken of," "to be the object of favor."[13] It also can mean "to celebrate with praises" and convey the sense of congratulations.[14] God will congratulate people who made faith-commitments to Jesus, charted the course of their lives by His principles and guidelines, and faithfully served Him. They had—and continued to have—God's approval. The phrase "blessed by my father" has the sense of "my father's blessed ones"—people who are His.[15] The phrase "inherit the kingdom" is an invitation to enter God's immediate presence for eternity. The redeemed placed themselves under God's sovereign rule in their lifetimes; at Jesus' return, they will live forever in His loving, beneficent presence. The kingdom to which Jesus referred has been prepared for the redeemed "from the foundation of the world." That is, God's eternal purpose always has been that people would experience saving relationship with Him. As far back as one can reach in eternity, God's purpose for people has been redemptive. People who receive His grace will experience the fulfillment of His intended blessing for all people.

We need to be clear that God is not and will never be partial or arbitrary. His arms, as it were, are open to receive all who repent and place faith in Christ. As Jesus made clear in the remainder of His depiction of final judgment, people pass judgment on themselves.

---

[13] *The Analytical Greek Lexicon*, p. 174.

[14] Joseph Henry Thayer, *A Greek-English Lexicon of the New Testament*, p. 259.

[15] Broadus, p. 509.

Jesus' Standard for Judgment
Matthew 25:35-36

The word "for" (verse 35) connects what follows with the believers' entrance into God's immediate presence in eternity. Jesus listed six actions the redeemed consistently took as they lived out their lives in relationship with Him. I cannot imagine the surprising, jarring effect of His words on the disciples who were listening to Him. In our terminology, their mouths must have flown open, and their eyes must have "bugged out." I think His words conveyed a tone of warning the disciples were to convey to people who would respond positively to their proclamation of the good news of available salvation.

For a long time, I have been impressed by the fact that nothing Jesus listed in His standard of judgment in Matthew 25 is religious in nature. He made no reference to synagogue or temple attendance, prayers, Scripture-study, tithing, or law-keeping. Instead, He listed everyday acts of kindness, of compassion. I believe His list was (and remains) representative, not exhaustive. The disciples must have exchanged startled looks as Jesus used as the basis of congratulations to believers their giving Him food, drink, hospitality, clothing, care during illness, and visits during imprisonment. Many of us look at His description of judgment and come away thinking that something about it is not right. Something is lacking. Then the thought strikes us: It is not "spiritual" enough; it is too human. It is too simple. Its components are bread, water, clothing, and care. Surely, we think, more is involved in judgment than what Jesus indicated.

John A. Broadus wrote that indeed more will be included in final judgment. He stated: "It would be a grave mistake to suppose that nothing will be regarded in the judgment, nothing help in determining a man's future, but the simple question whether he has been benevolent towards suffering Christians"[16] In my view, Jesus meant needy people regardless of their spiritual state. At any rate, compassionate acts will be a major component of final judgment.

Startled looks must have taken on an element of puzzlement with Jesus' emphasis that His genuine followers will have performed kind, gracious acts for *Him*. The disciples and others may have done some of the acts for Jesus, such as giving Him food and water, but most people had not done anything directly for Him. By far the largest majority of people who stand before Him at the last judgment will never have seen Him, much less will have ministered directly to Him. What did He mean? What Jesus did in Matthew 25:31-46 was to drive home a truth many of us had rather not hear—one we easily can try to alter, avert, or ignore. The foundational truth is that if we will not constantly strive to relate to other people, we cannot be rightly related to God. We are never given the option of choosing to follow Christ and to reject others. We may have the most profound theology, an enviable catalog of religious achievements, and a thorough knowledge of the Scriptures, but if these fail to affect our

---

[16] Broadus, p. 510.

responses to one another—to stimulate acts whose source is love—they are empty. An attitude that excludes people automatically excludes us from relationship with God. William Barclay wrote: "God's judgment does not depend on the knowledge we have amassed, or the fame that we have acquired, or the fortune that we have gained, but on the help that we have given."[17]

Jesus told His hearers—and goes on telling us—that what we do in positive response to one another is evidence of who we are. Acts of love (determined good will that works for others' welfare) and compassion do not establish a relationship with Him, but a person related to Him will perform acts of kindness that give solid evidence of that relationship. Our responses to people—especially to people in real need—reveal character, sensitivity, and genuineness.

Jesus gave a brief list of compassionate responses to Him, identifying Himself closely with needy people. First, genuine believers gave others food to alleviate their hunger. The Greek term Jesus used for "hungry" can mean "famished," desperately wanting food.[18] Jesus' committed followers realized hungry people needed food to survive and fed them. The word Jesus used for "something to eat" means "to eat bread," "to take the usual meal."[19] In Jesus' day, many people in His land lived on the edge, or as we sometimes say,

---

[17] William Barclay, "The Gospel of Matthew, vol. 2, in *The Daily Study Bible*, p. 359.

[18] *The Analytical Greek Lexicon*, p. 314.

[19] *The Analytical Greek Lexicon*, p. 168.

"from hand to mouth." Many depended on a day's wage to feed hungry families. Some days saw families dealing with stark hunger because the husband/father could not find work. That is the reason the temptation for Jesus to use His power to provide food for Himself—and beyond that, for the masses—was such a strong one. (See Matthew 4:1-3.) Jesus said His compassionate followers did what they could to feed hungry people.

As I write, our nation—and indeed, our world—is in the grip of a deadly pandemic. In our country, Covid 19 has caused widespread sickness, rapidly mounting deaths, and massive job loss. Suddenly, numerous families are in a place they never imagined they would be: waiting in long lines of cars to receive boxes of food from overwhelmed food banks. For some, food once taken for granted is now difficult to obtain.

My wife and I fall into the category of people who are severely threatened by the virus. Thus, we are reluctant to go outside unless to do so is absolutely necessary. We live close to three grocery stores. Before the deadly virus struck, we made frequent trips to buy food items we needed. Now, most often my wife places orders online to the nearest store, and an essential worker delivers the items to our door. I no longer take food for granted, and I no longer consider drivers of produce trucks and grocery-store employees to be non-essential. For Christ's followers, to help provide food to the hungry is both a responsibility and an opportunity to help. We cannot help everybody, but we can help somebody.

Second, Jesus' true followers noted others' thirst and gave them water (or wine). In the promised land in Jesus' day, good drinking water was not always readily available. To note others' thirst and to give them good water was no random act of kindness; it was a determined sharing of an absolute necessity. Most of us take clean water for granted, until a Flint, Michigan, happens—or until we are confronted with the truth that other places in the world are in desperate need of wells that produce clean water. Several years ago, a pastor from Myanmar (formerly Burma) spoke to a group in our church and stressed his people's desperate need of water wells. Our class of coed senior adults collected money for new wells, grateful for our access to clean water and wanting others to have access to it.

Third, Jesus' committed followers gave others hospitality; they opened their homes to others in need of shelter. In Jesus' land of the first century, good, safe places of lodging for travelers were scarce. Followers of Christ often provided other believers with places to stay as they journeyed. The word stranger could have the sense of a foreigner. In Jesus' day, "foreigners were quite often treated roughly."[20] Taking in a foreigner was an expression of extreme kindness. Today, most of us may be reluctant to open our homes to strangers. Yet opportunities for taking in strangers present themselves. One of these in my city is called "Room in the Inn."

---

[20] Herschel H. Hobbs, "Matthew/Mark" in *An Exposition of the Four Gospels*, vol. 1, p. 353.

As I was contemplating the possibility of writing on the subject of Jesus' words in Matthew 25:31-46, I sat with others gathered for our church's Sunday morning worship. On the order of worship, time was allotted for Father Charles Strobel to speak. I was elated, for he is one of my favorite people—a true servant of God and a tireless advocate for the poor and homeless of my city. He was present with us to thank our congregation for taking part in our city's ministry to the homeless. In doing so he briefly capsuled the history of what had become known as The Room in the Inn. He related how years before, a group of people had come to his church's parking lot one winter evening to set up for the night. He went out to talk with them and learned they were homeless and were looking for a safe place to spend the night.

Father Strobel invited the people into his church, fed them, and invited them to stay the night. As he anticipated, the group showed up the next night. Again, he opened his church to them, fed them, and provided space for them to spend the night. He realized that his church could not meet these people's needs alone. He began calling churches in the area, and four churches agreed to host groups of the homeless for overnight stays. Father Strobel said the thought came to him that people participating in the growing ministry were doing what people Jesus commended in Matthew 25 had done—extending practical care to the least of His brothers. At the time the compassionate priest spoke in my church, about 200 churches in our area were hosting the homeless during the cold winter months. I appreciated his affirmation of and appreciation for my church's contributions to the needed ministry. At the same time, I realized our efforts comprised a small drop in a big bucket. We cannot congratulate ourselves for doing what our Lord expects of us but must continue to seek ways to extend care to more of the needy.

Jesus' words in Matthew 25 constantly remind me that life is not measured by what we receive, acquire, or amass but by what we give. What is more, our lives are not measured by what people think of us but by what our Lord thinks of us.

Fourth, when Jesus was inadequately clothed, the people rightly related to Him gave Him needed garments. The word Jesus used for naked has a wide range of meanings. It could mean having no clothes at all. It could have the sense of lacking an outer garment and having only an inner garment to ward off the night's chill. In addition, it could indicate a person's being poorly clad, as being clothed in rags. At any rate, Jesus' people acted to provide the needy with adequate clothing.

As is the case with many churches, my church collects gently used, clean clothes that are made available to homeless people who attend our church or who come to the church asking for clothing. We call our storage room the Christ Closet. My wife and I are among many members who periodically contribute clean and gently used clothing. For a time, I felt pretty good about my gifts to this ministry. At intervals, I went through the items in my closet and selected ones I no longer wore or that were no longer in style. I took them to the church, thinking that at least some who needed clothing would have access to them. That gave me a sense of satisfaction.

My thinking suddenly changed one Sunday morning in a Sunday School Bible study session. We were discussing needs for the Christ Closet and our support of it when a faithful, insightful member said something I had not thought about. He pointed out that we could not congratulate ourselves too much. After all, we were providing *used* clothing; we seldom if ever made *new* clothes available. He strongly implied that we should do so. Now, when I contribute used clothes, I do so with the knowledge that I am doing the bare minimum. I am doing *something,* but not nearly enough.

Fifth, when individuals were sick, Jesus' true followers visited them. The word visited means much more than dropping by for a while. It has the senses of providing care, of tending. Jesus' parable of the good Samaritan is a vivid example of what He meant.

Sixth, Jesus' genuine followers were not reluctant to identify with people imprisoned, possibly because of their commitment to Him. If believers were the ones imprisoned, those who "visited" (literally, "came to") them faced the real danger of being incarcerated also.

A close look at Jesus' list of acts done for Him is informative, disturbing, and challenging. Notice that they are small, but they are highly significant. They have meaning because of what they reveal. The spectacular and noteworthy do not always offer the best measure of a person. Ordinary and commonplace acts—acts of compassion—often give the clearest indication of what a person really is at center. The acts that Jesus will congratulate people for having done fall within everyone's abilities. I can do them; you can do them. We cannot plead difficulty beyond our abilities or resources. We do not have to have scintillating talent to offer food; we do not have to be exceptionally intelligent to give a cup of cold water; we do not have to be magnetic personalities to extend fellowship to the unlovely, the ungracious, the undesirable. To give them, we only need to be sensitive and responsive to human need. Clearly, the importance of the acts Jesus listed does not lie in their size.

The actions Jesus listed certainly are not outstanding as we usually define noteworthiness. They seldom draw the spotlight or applause or praise. For the most part, they are not memorable. You will not find them listed in in tables of statistics, and they are not reported in denominational publications. Yet their significance remains: They reveal our true selves. They are expressions of character.

The six small acts are significant because of what they can do: They can have lasting impact. They can accomplish what the limited power of words cannot do. I know this truth firsthand. I was in a shabby, run-down section of New Orleans. The time was around noon on a typically hot, sticky summer day. As I went about my part-time job of delivering utility bills, I approached a rather rickety dwelling. As I slipped the bill under the sagging screen door, I heard the easily identifiable voice of an elderly black lady. She remarked on the heat of the day, then she asked: "Would you like some water?" I immediately had visions of uncleanliness, of a dirty glass and murky water. To be honest, I also thought of her blackness and my whiteness. I was still engaged in the difficult process of ridding myself of the racial prejudice so prevalent in the culture in which I grew up. Besides all that, I was in a hurry to complete my route. I declined her offer, thanked her, and went on my way.

I walked away from the gracious lady and her kind offer, but I have retained the memory and the jolting realization that came to me as I replayed the scene as I continued on my way. Soon, I was away from the kind lady and her house, but I have never been able to get away from the voice conveying a kind offer. She had no idea who I was, what quality person I might be. She only thought I might be thirsty, another human being whom she might help a little. That I was of a different race did not matter. She could expect nothing in return. No one else was around to take note. Later it came to me with force: She was doing what I was called on to do as Jesus' follower: offering to share what she had with someone who might need it. The incident probably faded from her memory, but I will always remember it. It continues to challenge me to help others out of what I have.

The small acts Jesus listed are significant because in the final analysis they are done to and for Him. He identifies with people who are the objects of His love and care. In his commentary on the Gospel of Matthew, William Barclay included two dramatic, moving illustrations of this truth.[21] The first illustration centered on the life-changing experience of Francis of

---

[21] Barclay, pp. 360-361.

Asissi. Francis was born to wealth and privilege. Yet he was unhappy because he felt something was lacking in his life. On one occasion he was riding in the countryside when he encountered a leper who displayed all the ugly evidences of his ravaging disease. Francis was moved by the man's devastating condition. He dismounted and enfolded the pitiful man in a warm embrace. As he did so, to him the man's face seemed to change to the face of Christ. Francis found his life's mission: to minister to leprosy's victims.

To me, Barclay's second illustration has proved to be unforgettable. It puts in dramatic terms the undeniable truth of Jesus' identifying with hurting humanity. Martin of Tours was a Roman soldier, and he was a Christian. On a cold winter day, he was entering a city when he encountered a beggar who was obviously painfully affected by the bitter cold. The beggar stopped Martin and pleaded for alms. Martin had no money to give. He removed his worn and frayed soldier's cloak. He cut it in half and gave one half to the beggar. That night Martin had a dream. In his dream he saw heaven. Jesus was surrounded by the angels, and He was wearing half a Roman soldier's cloak. One of the angels asked the reason Jesus was wearing such a tattered garment and wanted to know who had given it to Him. Jesus answered, "My servant Martin gave it to me."

Jesus singled out the small, simple acts that reveal true character, have enormous effect, and emphasize the truth that One who took on our humanity identifies with all humanity. His people exercise active care for others.

We do well to note that the acts Jesus listed are spontaneous in nature. They rise out of deep concern for people. They are performed out of what a person is; they are the natural outflow of a right relationship with God. They are the instantaneous responses of love to recognized need—what William Barclay called "help which is quite uncalculating."[22]

At this point, I must confess and repent. I am not always spontaneous in my response to need. I am working on it, but I am not quite there. Too often, when I am confronted with a need I can meet, I calculate the cost to me in terms of money, time, and effort. I struggle with inconvenience and interruptions in my schedules or plans. I am no model of what Christ expects, but by His grace I am making progress. What about you?

Arguably, the most vivid brush stroke on Jesus' remarkable canvas of people presented with their generous and closed attitudes and actions is the genuine surprise of the righteous. They did what they saw needed to be done because they cared. Jesus said they extended care to "the least" of His "brothers and sisters" (Matthew 25:40) and in doing so ministered to Him. Who were "the least" in the society of Jesus' day? These were society's marginalized and discounted, occupants of the lowest tier. In his paraphrase of Jesus' words, Eugene Peterson rightly used the words "overlooked and ignored" for the term "least."[23] They

---

[22] Barclay, p. 359.

[23] Eugene H. Peterson, *The Message: The Bible in Contemporary Language*, p. 1797.

were "the people of the land" and included the poorest of the poor, living on the edge. The sick and the maimed fell into this category. Who are "the least" in our society? High on the list are people who, through no fault of their own, cannot be productive, who cannot fend for themselves. They are the homeless and the hungry and the jobless and the helpless among us.

The people on Jesus' right hand had not even known that their Lord took note of the care they had extended to needy people. On the other hand, the darkest sweep on the canvas depicting judgment is the shock of the unrighteous at their lack of response to others in need. Jesus' words concerning what they failed to do must have been "like the falling of clods on the coffin."[24] In essence, they exclaimed: "If we had known these were important to you, we would have gladly done them." Their judgment lay in their failure to count people—all people—as of more worth than religious performance. In piling up religious credits, they had passed unseeingly those for whom Christ had died. They did this because they had never understood—or had never taken the time and made the effort to understand—the mind of the One whom they called Lord in pious tones.

Luke preserved a disturbing account that may be a penetrating parable, though some interpreters view it as an actual event. In 16:19-31, Jesus told about a rich man who lived lavishly and a poor, suffering man named Lazarus, who lay at the wealthy man's gate,

---

[24] Archibald Thomas Robertson, "The Gospel According to Matthew" in *Word Pictures in the New Testament*, vol. 1, p. 201.

longing for table scraps. At length, both men died. The rich man experienced torment in Hades, while Lazarus was at Abraham's side. Implied is the truth that the wealthy man's failure to help Lazarus revealed a severely flawed character that lacked compassion. He had passed Lazarus every day and failed to really see him. The poor man had become merely part of the scenery. The lesson for us is that we need to see people, especially people in need, and to act to help.

Jesus' priority must also be ours. People were, and remain, His priority. Of course, this truth is evidenced first by His coming to provide a way of grace into relationship with God for all people who will make faith-commitments to Him and will follow Him in faithful discipleship. Then, throughout His earthly ministry He made seeking the lost and ministering to people's needs His priority, and He did not allow Judaism's plethora of rules and regulations to get in His way.

To me, one of the most dramatic and emphatic evidences of people's importance to Jesus is an incident that occurred near the beginning of His public ministry. We are indebted to Mark for including it in his Gospel (Mark 3:1-6). I believe the event is representative of Jesus' consistent emphasis on the priority of people. His compassion for all people was at the center of His ministry.

According to Mark, Jesus entered the synagogue, likely in Capernaum. Among the assembled people was a man with "a shriveled hand" (3:1). Luke added that the man's right hand—likely his strongest hand—was affected. The religious leaders who opposed Jesus because He did not keep their Sabbath regulations in ministering to people's needs intently "eyed" Jesus to observe His response to the man. They were ready to pounce if He healed the man, for their burdensome interpretations of the Commandments included works forbidden on the Sabbath, and one of those works was making someone well. Those ministering to a sick person could stabilize the individual but could not make him or her well. What would Jesus do? If He healed on the Sabbath, the religious leaders were ready; they were poised to strike, prepared to charge Him with breaking the Commandment.

Jesus directed the unfortunate man to stand where everyone could see him. Likely He wanted everyone to see the man's condition and to witness the cure. Did He also make an appeal for compassion? Jesus posed a probing rhetorical question whose answer was that every day is a day to do good, and that included the Sabbath. He could have waited until the next day to heal the man because his life was certainly not in danger. Instead, Jesus insisted that human need demanded immediate response. To Jesus, waiting a day was to waste a day. The religious leaders had no answer.

To me, the next words in Mark's account are crucial and telling. In the silence following His penetrating question, Jesus looked at each religious leader in turn, and He looked at them "with anger" (3:5). I firmly believe we must reject the attempt to soften Jesus' strong response by calling it "righteous indignation." The word Mark used means "wrath"—something much more than the emotion of anger or rage. In the

New Testament, the term is frequently used to indicate God's determined, settled opposition to sin. Another Greek term has the sense of sudden fury that is ignited, burns fiercely, and dies down. I am convinced Jesus' response to the heartless religious leaders was an expression of His constant opposition to people's indifference to and lack of compassionate action on behalf of needy people.

Mark gave the reason for Jesus' strong reaction to what the religious leaders were doing. In "the hardness of their hearts" (Mark 3:5), they were using the afflicted man as an object to set up a test case for Jesus. Instead of viewing the man with compassion and welcoming any possibility of his healing, they were poised to accuse Jesus of breaking one of their Sabbath rules. Note that their lack of compassion also grieved Jesus. They failed to grasp God's care for every person.

Jesus instructed the man to stretch out his hand for all to see, and it was made whole. Instead of celebrating, the religious leaders left the synagogue determined to kill Jesus. Put in sharpest contrast is compassion for needy people over against preoccupation with religious rules and regulations. People matter much more than religious orthodoxy.

We could sift through the Gospels and list numerous incidents that demonstrate the priority Jesus placed on people. Repeatedly, He was moved with compassion because of people's plights. He felt with them so deeply that He acted of help them. Because of Matthew's account, professed Christians can never claim they did not know Jesus' priority and act on it.

Scattered throughout our history as a nation have been periods of crisis during which the rights and welfare of segments of our population were at stake. I firmly believe we have arrived at another such crisis. In the "haves' " frantic pursuit to attain or retain power, to protect positions of privilege, and to gain or increase wealth, people sometimes labeled "the have nots" are too often ignored or, even worse, exploited. To Jesus, every person was (and is) someone of worth. He affirmed every person's dignity. To conveniently keep putting out of mind or refusing to acknowledge the legitimate needs of the poor is to reject the priority Jesus placed on all people. To Him, our response is a serious matter. The righteous people's surprise at Jesus' words indicate they had not tabulated their helpful actions on behalf of the needy. Dietrich Bonhoeffer, in his classic book *The Cost of Discipleship*, wrote that serious followers of Christ can never be conscious of their good works. God alone knows our good works; we only know His good work of grace in us. When our response to the needy around us is spontaneous, we avoid the danger of a calculated goodness—a righteousness keenly aware of itself.

I should have known better, but I didn't. I do now, for I learned from the experience. He was an older pastor who had come to the seminary to further his education. I was young and green and more than a little tactless. He entered the dorm room where several students were talking. He spoke to an acquaintance and made a statement I considered to be a shade off-color and unnecessary. I indicated as much to him. He abruptly left the room, obviously irritated. Shortly, he was back, his anger at the point of exploding. As I recall, with his finger in my face his outburst went something like this: "Who do you think you are to correct me? If you ever do as much as I have for the Lord, then maybe you can do that. But I doubt you will ever do as much for the Lord as I have done." In the ensuing years, as I have reflected on his heated words, I have concluded that he probably was right in his assessment. Yet I am somewhat saddened that he used his works of ministry to put me in my place.

I am convinced that the moment we take pleasure in recounting to ourselves or to others our deeds and accomplishments for Christ, pumping up our egos is our full reward. In the Sermon on the Mount, Jesus said, "When you give to the poor, don't let your left hand know what your right hand is doing" (Matthew 6:3). For a long time, those words remained a puzzle for me. I have come to believe that Jesus was warning against retaining a mental catalog of our good deeds for others. In essence, He was saying: "Do what you can for the needy people in your path and move on to the next opportunity without making an entry in your ledger of good works." Love does not calculate or tabulate. Love responds to need in Jesus' spirit.

In an effort to be honest, I have a confession to make. I have difficulty resisting the temptation to be my own cheering section when I do something helpful for someone who cannot repay me and from whom I expect nothing in return. It is as though I am tempted to stand outside myself and applaud. A number of years ago, when I retired, I wanted to do something for people in need, people who could never pay me back. My church was engaged in The Room in the Inn ministry to homeless people during the cold winter months I mentioned earlier. Once a week we opened our recreation center as an overnight shelter for homeless men. I volunteered to arrive early the following morning to prepare the facility for its weekly regular use. Later, I helped prepare the center for soon-to-arrive homeless men. When I reflect on those acts, I remind myself that my decidedly small contributions were only what I should have done as Jesus' follower and can elicit no self-commendation.

Some people in New England grasped this truth, for they placed a plaque in the outside wall of Plymouth's High Street Chapel. The plaque's inscription recounts how John Pounds, a mender of shoes, gave out of his modest earnings to help feed, clothe, and educate hundreds of poor children. The last line of the plaque's inscription drives home Jesus' message: "Thou shalt be blessed—for they cannot recompense thee." My guess is that the thought never entered John Pounds' mind that his compassionate acts would be commemorated. Most likely, he never wanted or expected recognition for his selfless acts of compassion.

I often reflect on a contemporary example of compassionate action on behalf of suffering people. West of where I live, located on the Mississippi River, is the city of Memphis, Tennessee. Danny Thomas, a popular comedian of a past generation, was moved by the plight of children who suffered debilitating and often fatal diseases, especially childhood cancer. He established The St. Jude Children's Research Hospital to seek a cure for cancer. His daughter Marlo continues his work toward eradicating childhood cancer. Parents who bring their children to St. Jude incur no expense for travel, housing, food, or medical treatment. Although a statue of Danny Thomas is prominently displayed, I firmly believe he sought no recognition for his work, only the relief of desperate people's suffering.

Years ago, one of my pastors told of a personal experience that was both funny and sad. He and a man who had recently become a member of the church were walking through one of the church's halls and passed a display of plaques on a wall. The man asked what the plaques represented. The pastor replied that they were displayed to honor Sunday School teachers who faithfully served their Lord in their church through teaching. Later, the man came to the pastor and requested the opportunity to teach a class. Subsequently, he was enlisted to teach. A year later, he came to the pastor's office and asked the reason his plaque had not been posted on the wall of honor. Clearly, at least part of his motive for teaching—and evidently a large part—was his desire to be recognized. The drive for recognition well may lurk in too many of us. I have found that I often have to squelch it. The people Jesus will commend at the final judgment will be amazed that their compassionate acts had such profound meaning.

My guess is that not many of us are totally free from a carefully worked out goodness, the tendency to help people who can help us, to court the favor of individuals who can push us to the front of the line and boost us up whatever ladder to success we have chosen. Or we tend to help people with a view to ultimate reward. The reward of the helpful people in

Jesus' depiction of final judgment was the knowledge that life had been made somewhat easier and a little better for others who were needy. The givers expected no commendation; they merely did what was natural for them.

Jesus' depiction has a somber note: The presence or absence of the compassionate acts He listed have a separating quality. Performing these simple deeds gives evidence of relationship with Christ; failing to see needs and to move to meet them indicates a lack of such a relationship. The sobering truth is that this sifting process is going on now. In a real sense, every day is a day of judgment.

The presence or absence of compassionate acts for others separates people who have Jesus' standard of values from those who do not—individuals who see others as of supreme importance from those who do not—the concerned from the calloused—the sincere and genuine from the mere play-actors.

She was a woman of questionable reputation in a small town; thus, her chances of being accepted were slim and none. Besides, she was a mere taxi-driver. Most of the pious in the community avoided or merely tolerated her. Someone, however, cared enough to persuade her to attend the local Baptist church in the hope it would be a turning point for her. Her presence in a women's Sunday School class alarmed and offended some of the good ladies of the church. One irate saint threatened to leave the church if the woman came again. Not to worry. The woman never came again. I did not see her for years until after I came to New Orleans to attend seminary. In my part-time job of delivering utility bills for New Orleans Public Service, I went into all types of establishments. One day I delivered a bill to a bar on Decatur Street, and I saw her. She was highly intoxicated. My indictment is that I did not stop. Since that time, I have wondered whether her life might have been different and better had some people cared years ago when she showed an interest in righting her life. People matter—most of all.

"Lord, when did we see you hungry or thirsty or a stranger, or without clothes, or sick, or in prison, and not help you?" (Matthew 25:44). We see Him every day—in one another's faces, and in the faces of people who are hurting. I wonder how long it will take us to really understand. Will it be in the chilling words, "I tell you, whatever you did not do for one of the least of these, you did not do it for me"? (Matthew 25:44).

People who give no evidence of faithfully serving Jesus by serving others will go into eternity separated from Him. Whatever your concept of hell is—literal fire or the anguish of separation from God—Jesus made clear that condition was never meant for people, the highest of God's creation. God's intention from eternity has been that people accept His invitation of grace extended in Christ and enjoy never-ending relationship with Him. The choice is ours to make.

Addendum

We too easily can focus on getting. Through the years, when the subject of my most memorable Christmas has come up (and at random other times), my mind has gone to an unusual event in my childhood. For years, my favorite Christmas was the one when I received exactly what I asked for: a large ball and a red wood wagon. I was five years old, and in 1940 the country was not yet all the way out of the Great Depression. As I recall, the wood wagon cost five dollars—a hefty price at the time and was a challenge for my parents, who like most everyone else in my small town were scrambling to make a living. The wagon was beautiful, with green siding that could be added to form a seat if someone pulled it to give you a ride. I chose not to use the green sides and seat; instead, I propelled myself by placing one knee and leg in the wagon and by pushing with the other leg. The wagon gave me countless hours of pleasure—and wore out many pairs of shoes. When my father died in 1997, we found the wagon in his utility shed. It had remained largely intact for 57 years. The sight of it took me back across the years to a small boy's joyous Christmas— a happy time of getting.

As I grew older, I came to count another Christmas as the most memorable one—but not because of what I received. My father, mother, and I were eating our Christmas meal at mid-day. I do not remember how old I was, but I was still a child. In the apartment my parents rented, the kitchen also served as our dining area. Our table was situated in front of a window that looked out on a dirt road that ran from a city street down toward the railroad tracks. Beyond the road were the remains of what once had been a vast area for drying lumber produced by a large sawmill. As we ate, we saw a man walking down the road toward the tracks. His clothes and unkempt appearance gave evidence that he was a hobo headed for the passing of a slow-moving freight train. As I recall, my father was the one who suggested that we share our food with the man. My father quickly walked out on the house's side porch and called out to the man, inviting him to stop and eat. The man quickly did so. He walked into our yard, up the porch steps, and sat in one of the large chairs on the porch. My mother brought him a plate piled full of food When he finished eating, my parents offered him seconds. Then they offered articles of clothing. Finally, the man indicated he had all he could carry. We watched him walk to the road and continue down toward the tracks. We never saw him again, but we had a warm feeling of satisfaction that we had helped someone in need. None of us was aware of Jesus' words of commendation for helping others. I am grateful for the memory of that experience, but it also indicts me for not having done similar acts more often.

I struggle to move from being self-centered to serving others generously and consistently, and my guess is that I am not alone in that effort. One of my favorite and most cherished books is titled A Touch of Wonder by Arthur Gordon. Since I read it years ago—and later reread it—it has had a lasting impact on me. One paragraph continues to ring true for me: "Most of us spend our lives trying to escape from self-centeredness. Maybe that's the whole point, the whole challenge, what the whole thing is all about. Some of us succeed better than others. It seems to me that the ones who have most success are those who somehow turn self-caring into what might be called other-caring."[25] I continue to be in process.

---

[25] Arthur Gordon, *A Touch of Wonder*, p. 13.

Truths for Reflection

Interpreters have dated the writing of Matthew's Gospel as early as A. D. 55-60[26] and as late as sometime between A. D. 70 and A. D. 90.[27] Whatever the precise date, the important truth for our consideration is that Jesus' words in Matthew 25:31-46 have been available for study and reflection for centuries. At first people had limited access to the Scriptures, but through the years availability has increased to the point that almost anyone can have access to a Bible or a translation of the New Testament. That means most if not all of us can read and respond positively to Jesus' depiction of final judgment.

A dictionary definition of the term reflection is "serious thought; contemplation."[28] The word ponder is a suitable synonym, for it means "to weigh."[29] When we allow Jesus' words in Matthew 25 to really sink in, we become aware of profound truths.

The first truth I find is that Jesus issued a serious warning: correct theology (thinking about God) and sound religious beliefs and practices are not substitutes for compassion. Compassion is infinitely more than a benevolent emotion. Compassion is feeling with another that issues in action for the person's well-being. Compassion was an integral part of Jesus'

---

[26] Hobbs, p. 9.

[27] Stagg, p. 74.

[28] *Webster's New World Dictionary of the American Language*, p. 624.

[29] *Webster's*, p. 578.

character and must be a key element of ours. Words and good intentions are not nearly enough. We must be moved so deeply that we act to meet needs.

For many years, my favorite comic strip has been "Peanuts," created and cleverly written and drawn by Charles Shultz. Periodically, Shultz would weave biblical truths into a strip. In one strip, he pictured Snoopy, the dog, shivering in the snow. Two characters see him and decide to approach him to comfort him. They admonish him to be of good cheer, and they walk away. Snoopy is left with a large question mark above his head. Of course, Shultz presented a powerful depiction of James 2:15: "If a brother or sister is without clothes and lacks daily food and one of you says to them, 'Go in peace, stay warm, and be well fed,' but you don't give them what the body needs, what good is it?" Words are poor substitutes for benevolent actions. In fact, they are meaningless.

I think the second truth Jesus' words express is that they are meant to be vehicles of mercy and grace. Printed words cannot convey tone of voice. I believe Jesus' tone in addressing the "sheep" will be one of joy and delight. On the other hand, His tone in addressing the "goats" will convey grief. He will derive no satisfaction in their fate. They will have had ample opportunity to give open evidence of their relationship with Him. They will have had access to His words. As one of my seminary professors stated, Jesus' words were similar to a teacher giving in advance the answers to a final exam's questions.

As a sophomore in college, I learned a valuable lesson the hard way. The final exam in my physics course was approaching all too swiftly. The professor kindly listed a limited number of areas from which the exam would come. If we gave attention to those areas, we should do well. For some long-forgotten reason, I decided the professor probably would not include a couple of the areas he listed. To my dismay, he did. As a result, I almost failed the test. My failure to take the professor seriously cost me a letter grade.

Fast forward to a seminary classroom several years later. Class members faced a major exam. My church history professor wrote on a chalkboard a long list of questions from which he would make up the exam. If we prepared our answers to all the questions, we would ace the test. This time, I took the professor at his word. I worked hard and carefully prepared my answers. I did well on the exam because I took the teacher seriously.

My point is that to fail to take Jesus seriously about final judgement is to invite disaster. To take Him at His word and to live out our relationship with Him in compassionate service to others brings His commendation.

Carefully reading Jesus' words and letting them sink in, we can evaluate ourselves honestly. If we have not made needy people a priority and acted to help, we have time to repent and refocus. As has been correctly noted, none of us can help everyone, but you and I can help someone or several someones. For some of us, turning from concentration on ourselves to compassionate consideration of others is not easy. Doing so, however, reflects our Lord's character, which has to be our overriding purpose.

For centuries, Jesus' words in Matthew 25 have offered opportunities for people to take Him seriously. The words have given everyone who reads them the chance to value one another and to extend needed help in the Lord's spirit. Our response will form an integral part of our judgment. Extended life with Christ hinges, in large part, on whether we take His words seriously—or not. Not to take Him seriously eventually will issue in the ultimate surprise.

Selected Bibliography

Barclay, William, "The Gospel of Matthew," vol. 2, in *The Daily Study Bible* (Philadelphia: The Westminster Press, nd)

Bonhoeffer, Dietrich, *The Cost of Discipleship* (Second Edition, SCM Press Ltd, 1959)

Blomberg, Craig L., "Matthew" in *The New American Commentary*, vol. 22 (Nashville, Tennessee: Broadman Press, 1992)

Broadus, John A., "Commentary on the Gospel of Matthew" in *An American Commentary on the New Testament* (Valley Forge, Pa.: The American Baptist Publication Society, 1886)

Buttrick, George A., "The Gospel According to St. Matthew" in *The Interpreter's Bible* (Nashville: Abingdon Press, 1951)

Gordon, Arthur, *A Touch of Wonder* (Old Tappen, New Jersey: Pillar Books for Fleming H. Revell Company, 1974)

Hobbs, Herschel H., "Matthew/Mark" in *An Exposition of the Four Gospels,* vol. 1 (Grand Rapids, Michigan: Baker Books, 1996)

Holman Illustrated Bible Dictionary (Nashville Tennessee: Holman Bible Publishers, 2003)

Howard, Fred D., "The Gospel of Matthew: A Study Manual" in *Shield Bible Study Series* (Grand Rapids, Michigan: Baker Book House, 1961)

_____, "Matthew (Part 2)" in *Bible Book Study Commentary, July, August, September 1988* (Nashville, Tennessee: Convention Press)

Peterson, Eugene H., *The Message: The Bible in Contemporary Language* (Colorado Springs, Colorado: NavPress, 2002)

Robertson, Archibald Thomas, "The Gospel According to Matthew" in *Word Pictures in the New Testament,* vol. 1 (Nashville, Tennessee: Broadman Press, 1930)

Stagg, Frank, "Matthew" in *The Broadman Bible Commentary,* vol. 8 (Nashville, Tennessee: Broadman Press, 1969)

Thayer, Joseph Henry, *A Greek-English Lexicon of the New Testament* (Grand Rapids, Michigan: Zondervan Publishing House, 1970)

The Analytical Greek Lexicon (New York: Harper & Row Publishers, nd)

Tolbert, Malcomb O., *Good News from Matthew: A Layman's Commentary on the Gospel of Matthew,* vol. 2 (Nashville, Tennessee: Broadman Press, 1975)

Vincent, Marvin R., "The Gospel of Matthew" in *Word Studies in the New Testament,* vol. 1 (Grand Rapids, Michigan: Wm. B. Eerdmans Publishing Company, 1965)

Webster's New World Dictionary of the American Language (Nashville, Tenn.: The Southwestern Company, 1961)

www.ingramcontent.com/pod-product-compliance
Lightning Source LLC
Chambersburg PA
CBHW071409070526
44578CB00002B/528